THE HOMEMADE MILLIONAIRE'S

SECRETS OF THE RICH AND FREE

By the Best Selling Author of
The Parable of the Homemade Millionaire

Bryan

Featuring a Foreword by Tracey C. Jones,
President of Tremendous Life Books

James

K
PUBLISHING

"The Books You Need to Succeed"
332 Center Street • Wilkes-Barre, PA 18702
www.KallistiPublishing.com

The Millionaire's Message: The Homemade Millionaire's Secrets of the Rich and Free. Copyright © 2015 by Bryan James. All rights reserved. No part of this book may be reproduced or transmitted in any form or by any means, electronic or mechanical, including photocopying, recording, or by any information storage and retrieval system, without permission in writing from the publisher, except by a reviewer, who may quote brief passages in review.

Kallisti Publishing's titles may be bulk purchased for business or promotional use or for special sales. Please contact Kallisti Publishing for more information.

Kallisti Publishing and its logo are trademarks of Kallisti Publishing. All rights reserved.

Please note that any errors, typographical or otherwise, are here for a purpose: some people actually enjoy looking for them and we strive to please as many people as possible. If you would like to report a typo or error, please contact us via our web site. We'll make a the correction for future editions—and maybe reward you with a small gift.

ISBN-13 978-0-9848162-7-9

Library of Congress Control Number: 2014955816

DESIGNED & PRINTED IN THE UNITED STATES OF AMERICA

Table of Contents

Foreword i
Keeping the Code 1
   It Couldn't Be Done 6
All Things Are Possible 7
   If 17
Maximize Your Brain Power 19
Convincing Others 41
   The Race 50
The Power of Commitment 53
Little Things Mean a Lot 61
   The Winds of Fate 72
Nobility 73
About the Author 88

This book is dedicated to the heroines in my life: Jeanne, Karen, Ruth, Jean, Lois, Janet, Laura, and Lisa

Foreword

Almost ten years ago, my father, Charlie "Tremendous" Jones, wrote the foreword for *The Parable of the Homemade Millionaire*, Bryan James's first book. So it's perfectly fitting that me to write the foreword to Mr. James's new book, the one that you hold in your hands, *The Millionaire's Message*.

One quote for which my father is most known is "You'll be the same person in five years as you are today except for the books you read and the people you meet." *The Millionaire's Message* is one of those books that will change you. And Michael Zors, whom you will meet in the book, is a person you will be glad to meet.

Today's world is a veritable cornucopia of opportunity and happiness for anyone willing to reach out and get it. Or, to be more specific, for anyone who knows what it takes to get it.

Through the story of Michael Zors and his wife Ruth, you will learn that all things are indeed possible; how to maximize your brain power; the skill to persuade others; about the true power of commitment; and how it's the little things that add up to the big things in our lives.

Each of those, when learned and then practiced dutifully, build a life of success, happiness, and all good things.

Life doesn't have to be, nor should it be, drudgery. It can and should be about discovering your highest dreams and ideals.

Thankfully, people like Bryan James write books like this, books that remind us and teach us about the life that's possible — and attainable.

So settle yourself in your comfy chair and imbibe *The Millionaire's Message.* And don't worry about that feeling you'll have when you're finished. That's just your mind preparing its plans for you to take advantage of the new opportunities and goals in your life!

Tremendously yours…

Tracey Jones,
President of Tremendous Life Books, Speaker, and Author of *Beyond Tremendous: Raising the Bar On Life*

THE
MILLIONAIRE'S
MESSAGE

1
Keeping the Code

Ruth looked across the breakfast table at her husband. "You've been looking tired, Zors," she said. Zors is what everyone called Michael Zors, even his wife. "Is everything all right?"

"Sure," he said. "I just have a lot on my plate." Wordlessly, he held up his breakfast plate overflowing with eggs, sausage, and fruit. Zors always thought he was funnier than he really was.

"I'm serious," she said. "I know you, and I think something's wrong."

"You're way too smart for your own good. There is something bothering me, and I've been planning to ask for your help. I'm afraid, though, that you won't be thrilled by what I am asking."

"You can't have a pet monkey, Zors," Ruth kidded.

"Good one," Zors chuckled. "You know that's not what I'm talking about." Zors' face grew serious. "Ruth, we need to break the code of silence. I can't think of any other way to cope with the dilemma I'm facing." Zors' fork probed at his eggs.

"No, Zors. We're not going to break the code of silence. I don't know what your dilemma is," Ruth pulled her chair closer to the kitchen table, "but that's not an option. Let's discuss this problem of yours, and see if we can find a solution."

"Okay," he said. "Here it is in a nutshell. You know I feel the commitments I make to myself are sacred, right? And I never make commitments I can't keep. Well, the self-promise I made years ago, when it was manageable, has now grown to where it isn't. I need your help to keep that commitment."

"Zors, I'm always more than willing to help you, you know that."

"I do."

"So how does breaking the code of silence solve anything?"

"Okay, fair question. Let me answer it in this way. My commitment was to always be available to advise any sincere person on the success techniques you had taught me. But now it's gotten to the point where I've created quite a following. I'm peppered with requests for advice from dawn to dusk. I always enjoy these opportunities. But this, while at the same time trying to run our company, means I no longer have time to help everyone. I don't even have time to play golf anymore."

Ruth got the toast from the toaster and set it by his plate. "So where do I come in?"

Zors wagged his fork. "Well, if I can break the code and reveal to everyone that you're the real source of all my knowledge on how to be successful, then you can help me with all these requests for advice."

Ruth was quiet for a long moment. The kitchen clock ticked away the time. "Zors," she said finally. "That won't work. You know I'm not interested in the limelight. But I'd jump in if I believed it would solve your problem. It won't." Her hand closed on his. "You're caught in a positive spiral. The more you give, the more you create opportunities to give. All these people see you as a caring, giving, self-made millionaire who's exposed them to some highly effective success techniques."

"So?"

"So if I join in, the requests would increase to a deluge, and both of us would be buried! Zors, for starters, you are underestimating yourself. I know in the beginning I shared all the basic success systems my father used to build his empire. But through all your years of using and teaching them, you've not only become an expert, you've developed many innovations of your own."

"Smart man, your dad," Zors said, reaching for a slice of toast.

"And so are you. You are a great communicator."

"What about my jokes?"

"Eat your toast."

"You don't like my jokes?"

"Many people do," she said tactfully.

"Many people?" he responded. "Everyone!" His smile died away. "Ruth, I see no other answer."

"Now there's an affirmation that will serve you well," she said. "Of course there is another answer. A better answer. You're a time management expert, right?"

"Right."

"So we need to apply some of your expertise."

Zors shoved his plate aside. "Time management. Let me think a bit."

Ruth knew it wouldn't take long. She watched his smile break like sunshine.

"Out with it," she said.

"Here it is. Most of the questions I get each day are the same ones. Ten different people will ask me the same question. I have to answer it ten times. If I were talking to all those people at the same time, I would only have to answer it once."

"So what are you going to do," Ruth asked, "text message everyone?"

"No," Zors laughed. "I'm going to get them all in the same room at the same time. I'll book a small banquet room at the hotel once a month for a short talk. Then I can answer all their questions." Zors leaned back in his kitchen chair. "When people ask me questions during the month, I'll tell them they have to bring their questions to the monthly meeting to get an answer."

"Ah," said Ruth, clearing away the plates.

"It won't take me long to get them into a routine. They'll stop calling me all the time and just wait for the meeting." Zors had a flash of insight. "They can bring their spouses and friends if they wish. How about that? Actually, it could be a lot of fun."

"Great idea," Ruth said, excitement in her voice. "You know, it might be wise to charge per person"

"Yeah like ten dollars. How's that?"

Ruth nodded. "They'd value the information that way."

"What do we do with the money?"

"Enroll you in a keep fit class."

Zors grinned at her. "How about our charitable trust?"

"How about we go live in the Bahamas?"

"The charitable trust it is."

The kitchen clock ticked in the quiet. "I don't know what I would do without you, Ruth."

Zors started a program of regular monthly meetings. It wasn't long before he had to book a bigger room to accommodate the ever-growing crowds. This book captures what occurred at these meetings.

It Couldn't Be Done

Somebody said that it couldn't be done,
But he with a chuckle replied
That "maybe it couldn't," but he would be one
Who wouldn't say so till he tried.
So he buckled right in with a trace of a grin
On his face. If he worried he hid it.
He started to sing as he tackled the thing
That couldn't be done, and he did it.

Somebody scoffed: "Oh, you'll never do that;
At least no one ever has done it;"
But he took off his coat and he took off his hat,
And the first thing we knew he'd begun it.
With a lift of his chin and a bit of a grin,
Without any doubting or quiddit,
He started to sing as he tackled the thing
That couldn't be done, and he did it.

There are thousands to tell you it can't be done,
There are thousands to prophecy failure;
There are thousands to point out to you, one by one,
The dangers that weight to assail you.
But just buckle in with a bit of a grin,
Just take off your coat and go do it;
Just start to sing as you tackle the thing
That "cannot be done" and you'll do it.

–Edgar A. Guest–

2
ALL THINGS ARE POSSIBLE

Welcome and thank you for being here. I'm anxious to share some thoughts with you this evening, even my deepest thoughts. For instance, today I have been thinking a lot about how I would like to die—if I had a choice. I have decided that I would like to die the way my grandfather died, at peace in his sleep. Of course, the people he was driving in the car at the time were screaming pretty loudly, but he was at peace.

But unless we died a heroic death, it isn't about how we died, is it? It's more about how we lived, and even more important, how we are living now. Maybe, each day, if we make sure we are truly living life, as opposed to just reacting to it, everything else just might fall into place.

I am sure by now you all know that I believe five percent of the people in the world are the leaders who make the world function the way it does. Of course, if this is valid, then the other ninety-five percent are just going along for the ride. It follows then that if you are not a five percenter, you probably are just reacting to life, not actively living in it. Let me tell you a little story…

A few weeks ago I was golfing with my neighbor. I use the term *golfing* very loosely because he is a very challenged golfer. On the fifth hole he hit his ball into the rough and, when he found it, he discovered that it was sitting atop an anthill. He perceived this as a fortuitous event, since it was as if someone had teed the ball up for him. He took out his five iron, set his feet, and swung with all his might.

Unfortunately, he completely missed the ball, but hit the anthill dead on. He probably killed, I don't know, a thousand ants. Determinedly he swung again with the same results—missed the ball, killed another one thousand ants. After three more swings, and three more direct hits on the anthill, there were but two ants left who had survived the onslaught. One of the ants turned to the other and said, "If we want to get out of this alive, we better get on the ball!"

That is what I want to say to the ninety-five percenters. If you really want to live a life of fulfillment, you better get on the ball.

When I use the phrase, "Get on the ball," I am certainly not trying to insult anyone. I am not talking about effort or commitment; I am referring to the way we think. I will explain this by telling you about a very special person. To do so, I need to take you back to my youth.

I was a war baby—born during World War II. As a young boy in the late 1940s and early 1950s, I was an avid sports fan. I was particularly fascinated by track and field, especially the mile run. You see, at that time, no human being had ever run the American mile in under four minutes. *In the history of the world,* no one had been timed breaking that barrier.

There were magazine and newspaper articles back then suggesting that it might not be humanly possible to accomplish this feat. There had been thousands of middle distance runners who had trained for years who never got close. No, back then, it was widely believed that it just couldn't be done. There was, however, one runner who didn't seem to get the message.

On May 6, 1954, an Englishman, Roger Bannister, ran a one-mile race at Oxford, England. He completed the mile in three minutes, fifty-nine and four-tenths seconds, smashing the world's record and becoming the first human to break the four-minute mile!

This accomplishment amazed the world. Years later *Sports Illustrated Magazine* rated Banister's breakthrough, along with the scaling of Mount Everest, as the most athletic feats in the twentieth century. While I too was impressed, something else amazed me even more.

On June 21, 1954, less than two months after Bannister's extraordinary feat, an Australian, John Landy, ran the mile in three minutes, fifty-eight seconds flat—breaking Bannister's world record and becoming the second human to run a sub four-minute mile. Over the next few years, several other runners accomplished the feat and, as of today, hundreds of men have broken the four-minute mile.

How is all this possible? In the history of the world no one was able to accomplish this goal, but once someone did it, the dam burst and a flood of runners were successful in this undertaking.

The answer, my friends, is in the mental aspect involved in accomplishing great things. You see, it wasn't just a one- time event for Roger Bannister that sets him apart from everyone else; he continued to excel his entire life. He became an internationally known neurologist who made major contributions in his field. He introduced new procedures in the field of autonomic failure, an area of neurology focusing on illness characterized by certain automatic responses of the nervous system. He was the first recipient of *Sports Illustrated Magazine's* Sportsman of the Year Award. He was the first chairman of the Sports Council (now known as Sport England) and in 1975 was knighted by the Queen for all his contributions. He was able to accomplish all this because of how he viewed life. He did not limit himself by what others had done; he stayed focused on his goals—even if others thought them impossible.

Unfortunately, there are many who are happy to function within parameters established by those around them. They feel if they are about as productive as most of their peers, then they are living a satisfactory life. They generally become ninety-five percenters because, if they emulate everyone else, they have ninety-five chances out of one hundred of becoming ninety-five percenters.

We can learn a lot about how this type of thinking can limit us by studying fleas. A scientist put a number of fleas in a shallow aquarium to observe their behavior. He immediately had a problem, as the aquarium was five inches high with no top. Since fleas are excellent jumpers—they can jump up to seven inches—they were able to elevate above the sides of the aquarium and escape. So the scientist put screening over the top of the container. Immediately thereafter, the fleas jumped and bashed their little heads into the screened top. It didn't take long before they limited their jumping to just below the top. The interesting part is when the scientist took off the screening, the fleas were still jumping below where the top had been. *They had become programmed to jump lower than their potential.*

Many of us live our lives with perceived limits on what we can accomplish; just like those fleas, we have become programmed to function within parameters that are well below our potential. We are constantly measuring what we believe is possible for us to do by what others have done. In doing this we have about a five percent chance of modeling our behavior after someone who is truly successful. That means that ninety-five percent of the time we are focusing on mediocrity. We need to shake up the way we perceive in order to excel. This next story will give us a clue as to how this can be done.

Rick owned a successful company, but had been experiencing limited growth over the last three years. He had ten salespeople who sold about one million dollars each of product each year. This accounted for ten million dollars of revenue annually, which needed to be increased. Rick believed stagnant growth was a danger sign because "if you weren't growing, you were dying."

One way Rick could increase sales was to have additional salespeople to establish additional territories. A study of the numbers, however, didn't make this too appealing. Each new salesperson would not only require a salary, but also benefits and travel expenses. Rick calculated that it would take about two and one-half years for the territory to be developed to where income would meet expenses.

Rick concluded that the answer was to get his existing sales staff to sell more product. He was paying each about sixty thousand dollars per year, but spent another thirty thousand per salesperson in travel expenses. He would pay them more if they sold more, but they were working pretty hard already.

As Rick studied the situation, one surprising fact jumped out at him. *All his salespeople sold about the same amount of product each year.* There was only a 7 percent difference in total sales between his top salesperson and the bottom one, and that was over a two-year period. In other words, they were all quite content to sell about one million dollars per year and not much more. There was no laggard in the group, but there was no superstar either. This just didn't make sense.

One day in late October, Rick called a meeting of his sales staff. He announced that their annual salary increases, which took effect every January, would no longer be given to them. He was replacing this automatic raise with an incentive program, and the program was quite simple. Anyone who sold two million dollars or more of product in the next calendar year would receive a fifty thousand dollar bonus!

Initially, this announcement was not well received. When the salespeople met later, they complained to one another that Rick was not being fair. He had to know that it was impossible to sell two million dollars of product in one year, so he was really saying that no one was getting a raise. They were angry.

A week later, while the sales people were still grumbling, a legitimate discussion emerged. One salesman thought he could increase sales by making calls earlier in the day and later in the afternoon. He could then do his paperwork after hours, when his clients were not available. By doing this he thought he could increase sales by as much as forty percent. He would be almost halfway there. The others wanted to know why he was even considering it.

"A $50,000 bonus would change my life," he said. "I could pay off the mortgage on my house!"

Another salesperson chimed in with, "I could establish a serious college fund for my kids."

Soon they all had a vision of how this bonus could affect them in a significant way.

As the discussion continued over the next couple of weeks, they jointly created a workable plan to give them each a legitimate shot at the bonus. By changing their call patterns to call on clients with big dollar potential, they had a real chance.

Rick got his sales people to think differently. They had to re-examine the possibility of doing the impossible because the reward for doing so was life-changing. He caused them to focus on the outcome and then, back to the solution. That next year three salespeople earned a $50,000 bonus. Overall sales went from $10,000,000 to $17,000,000, so those three $50,000 bonuses were well worth it. In fact, Rick was so pleased with the results that he gave significant bonuses to the rest of his sales staff as well.

It is absolutely amazing how creative our minds can be once we learn how to awaken this creativity. By focusing on the goal and committing to it, our minds are forced to find a way. You will be absolutely astounded as to the creative power of your brain once you successfully awaken it.

Don't worry that something has never been done before. There are thousands of great accomplishments achieved each day, and they weren't by accident. By properly utilizing your fantastic mind, all things are possible.

—

Zors: Now, are there any questions?

Question: Zors, surely you don't mean that *all things* **are possible. Maybe some things or a lot of things, but not all things.**

Zors: So what is your question?

Question: That is my question. Let me ask it this way. Are all things really possible?

Zors: Funny you should ask. Yes, I believe all things are possible; it's just a matter of time and will. Let me explain it another way. In 1896 a women's group in Cleveland, Ohio was celebrating the one hundredth anniversary of the founding of the city. As part of the celebration, they created a time capsule to be opened at the two hundredth anniversary. When the capsule was opened in 1996, there were many interesting items. For me the most enlightening were two questions the women of eighteen ninety-six asked the future women of 1996. They asked if the railroad finally went across the entire United States, and if anyone had reached the North Pole.

Can you imagine that—a railroad across the country and reaching the North Pole? Why, we have gone to the moon and can fly across the country in a matter of hours! Those questions weren't asked because, to the women of 1896, those things were impossible. In their lives, no one had ever flown in a heavier- than-air vehicle, so the moon and flying across the country were inconceivable—impossible. Nothing is impossible, young man; it's just a matter of time and will.

Question: Zors, what happens if you shoot for the moon and fail? I mean, how do you continue to try to accomplish the impossible if you never make it?

Zors: As Yoda told us, "There is no try—you do or do not." It's like the football coach said: "We didn't lose the game, we just ran out of time."

If you run out of time and do not accomplish your mission, you probably aren't doing it correctly. Your mind is so powerful, there is really no excuse for failure. So shoot for the moon and reach your goal. The process of stimulating your creative subconscious, and those lessons you will learn on the way, are life-changing unto themselves, but are only some of the blessings of accomplishing greatness.

Question: Why is success so difficult that only 5-percent of the people attain it?

Zors: Success isn't difficult, it is easy. You see, there isn't really much competition out there. All you have to do is learn what the five-percenters do, and then get into the habit of consistently doing those things. That alone will put you ahead of about 95-percent of the population.

If

If you can keep your head when all about you
Are losing theirs and blaming it on you;
If you can trust yourself when all men doubt you,
But make allowance for their doubting too:
If you can wait and not be tired by waiting,
Or, being lied about, don't deal in lies,
Or being hated don't give way to hating,
And yet don't look too good, nor talk too wise;

If you can dream—and not make dreams your master;
If you can think—and not make thoughts your aim,
If you can meet with triumph and disaster
And treat those two imposters just the same:
If you can bear to hear the truth you've spoken
Twisted by knaves to make a trap for fools,
Or watch the things you gave your life to broken,
And stop and build 'em up with worn-out tools;

If you can make one heap of all your winnings and
    risk it on one turn of pitch—and—toss,
And lose, and start again at your beginnings,
And never breathe a word about your loss:
If you can force your heart and nerve and sinew
To serve your turn long after they are gone,
And so hold on when there is nothing in you
Except the will which says to them: "Hold on!"

If you can talk with crowds and keep your virtue,
Or walk with kings—nor lose the common touch,
If neither foes nor loving friends can hurt you,
If all men count with you, but none too much:
If you can fill the unforgiving minute
With sixty seconds' worth of distance run,
Yours is the earth and everything that's in it,
And—which is more—you'll be a man, my son!

–Rudyard Kipling–

3

Maximize Your Brain Power

Welcome and thank you for being here. I'm anxious to share some thoughts with you this evening. In fact, I am going to reveal a methodology to you tonight that is the most dynamic process I have encountered in my lifetime. It is so effective that, if you are not presently using it and you make the commitment to do so, your opportunities for success will soar. It involves increasing the use of an asset you presently have in your possession.

Let's assume that the furnace in your home is not working properly. A furnace repairman assesses the situation and announces to you that the furnace is functioning at twenty percent of its capacity. I am sure you would tell him to repair it, because if it is only functioning at twenty percent, then it is broken. If you took your car to a mechanic and he told you it was operating a twenty percent of its capacity, you would tell them to fix it, as it is obviously broken.

There is one asset you have, however, that if you could get it to function at the twenty percent level, you would be miles ahead of everyone else. That asset is your mind—your brain.

Experts tell us people use about five to ten percent of their brainpower. If that is true, then we are all wasting ninety to ninety-five percent of our brainpower. Since all of us who are here tonight are pretty smart, let's give ourselves the benefit of the doubt and say we are all at the ten percent level. Still, as smart as we are, we are wasting ninety percent of our most important asset.

But wait a minute. That means we have ninety percent to work with, so getting to the twenty percent level should not be that difficult. We only need to capture another ten percent of the ninety we are wasting.

Think about it—if we got to the twenty percent level, we would be twice as productive, twice as effective, and probably twice as successful as everyone else. And what if we only get to the fifteen percent level— we are still fifty percent ahead of everyone. Why, only twelve percent puts us twenty percent ahead. How do we get to twelve, fifteen, or even twenty percent?

The hardest part of getting to the twenty percent level is understanding that we are not there, and how wasteful that is. Can you imagine the waste involved in using your computer as a word processor and nothing else? Think about that for a minute; you use your computer each day as a word processor because you never knew it could do anything else! Finally, one day, someone shows you all the other applications possible with your computer. Can you imagine how exciting that would be? And think how much more you can accomplish using all those applications.

Well, that is what it is like for many people in the use of their minds. Since they really do not understand how dynamic and powerful their brains are, they are trapped in their struggle through life using maybe ten percent of its potential. Wouldn't their lives become greatly enriched if they began using twelve, fifteen, twenty percent, and more of this amazing asset?

That is what I will be discussing tonight—increasing your life's accomplishments by unleashing a heightened level of brainpower. Before we get into this fascinating topic, let me preface it by exploring a related concept.

There are many ways in which we can categorize ourselves and others. We can be introverts or extroverts, optimists or pessimists, those who have a need for accomplishment as opposed to those who have a need for affiliation, and so it goes. The concept I want to discuss tonight is locus of control, because we are people who have an internal or external locus of control. The normally isn't too much of a gray area here.

A person with external locus of control believes his life is controlled by outside forces; his boss, his spouse, his kids, his neighbors, his church and many others. He thinks that his ability to deal with these external elements determines how successful he will be.

A person with internal locus of control, however, believes that he is in control of his own life and success. He believes that he can accomplish his goals no matter what others think and do. He knows there will be obstacles, but he also knows he will overcome them and complete his mission. He takes full responsibility for his setbacks and his successes.

Experts tell us that, generally, people with internal locus of control are happier, more productive, and more successful than those with external locus of control. That is because living with an external locus of control means your life is out of control. You are at the mercy of everyone else's moods and desires, which in itself is a very stressful way to exist. This is why we need to have an internal locus of control, so from this point on, I want all of you to have an internal locus of control. Come on, flip the switch and do it!

I am noticing that you are all looking at me as if I were completely out of my mind. You know it isn't that easy. You cannot just flip a switch and change your core beliefs. If you truly believe those external forces control your path in life, then it is quite difficult to alter that belief overnight.

What if there were a mechanism that would allow you to complete any task quickly and correctly every time, and allowed you to reach any goal you desired? If you did have this tool, used it for a while and discovered it always worked, then your perspective would change, wouldn't it? Since you would know that you can accomplish the most difficult tasks and realize your greatest dreams, you would automatically become a person of internal locus of control. Today I will share this amazing technique with all of you.

Let's say that I asked to spend the day with you to observe how you function in the business world. If you agree, I promise to reward you for your efforts. When you consent, I meet you early the next morning at your home. I jump in your car and off we go.

I don't say much during the day, as I'm continually making notes on the clipboard I brought with me. When we finally get back to your house that evening, I thank you for allowing me to tag along. "As promised," I say, "I owe you a reward, and I will make good on that promise right now.

"During the time I spent with you today, I saw forty-two blue shirts. Every time I spotted a blue shirt, I made a note on my clipboard of where I saw it, what kind of shirt it was, who was in it, etc. Since you had the same opportunity to observe what I observed, I will give you a hundred dollars for every blue shirt that you saw and I can verify on my list."

This reward process probably would be a disappointment to you, because you wouldn't remember many blue shirts. Think about it: how many blue shirts did you see driving over here tonight? Blue shirts are the last thing you had on your mind tonight, and the same would be true if you spent the day with me. Blue shirts were not important to you, so you would probably only remember two or three that you observed during the day. You recalled three shirts, so I gave you three hundred dollars. Obviously, you would be disappointed. I mean, let's be serious; having to endure the pain of spending the day with me is worth a lot more than three hundred dollars.

"Okay, I will make it up to you," I would say. "Let's do this tomorrow with one major difference. This time you will know in advance that each blue shirt is worth one hundred dollars. I will have a pocket full of hundred dollar bills and pay you as we go!"

We would again start out early the next morning, but this time you would see blue shirts. You would see them in front of you, behind you, going in the other direction, and people walking, driving, or standing on the corner. We probably never would go into your office, as you would probably drive to a mall and walk around all day looking for blue shirts.

Under this scenario you would have pointed out seventy-eight blue shirts and you have seven thousand eight hundred dollars in your pocket! The first day you made three-hundred dollars, but the second, seven-thousand-eight-hundred. You did this only because you knew each shirt was worth a hundred dollars—you were supersensitive to spotting those shirts.

I shared this little scenario with you because that is exactly how our minds work. Since this is the communication age, we are literally barraged with data. We are so inundated by information that we really cannot consciously deal with all of it. Out of necessity, our brilliant minds have created a filter to let in only the important stuff. This filter is your subconscious mind, that lets in only the information that the subconscious believes is important to you. So, conversely, this internal receiver blocks out all other information it believes to be unimportant.

Please note that I stated that the subconscious mind lets through information it believes is important, while blocking information it believes is unimportant. The subconscious, however, can be wrong in its belief. It may be allowing information to reach the conscious mind that was important to us at one time, but not now. Also, we may have erroneously programmed our subconscious to let through data we believed to be important, but never really was. At the same time, we could be blocking information that is critical to our quest to reach our goals and dreams.

Yes, we all have a need to reprogram our subconscious minds. We all have a need to reevaluate what we are allowing into our consciousness and what we are blocking. Just like the blue shirts, there is valuable information to which we are being exposed, that we never consciously embrace. This information could be critical to our success and happiness, but since the subconscious doesn't know its importance, it never is realized consciously. Reprogramming will open up our conscious awareness to the truly important data now missing from our consciousness. Let's talk about the reprogramming process by first discussing the subconscious mind.

You are all somewhat familiar with the terms left brain and right brain, so I will not spend a lot of time talking about them. The only point I want to make is that right-brained people often think in pictures. Also, many young children are often right-brained at an early age of development, so when you tell them something, they see it as a picture in their minds.

When you say to a child, "don't run," he sees a picture of himself running. There is no picture for don't. I know a teacher who deals with this problem by telling the students to use their walking feet—a different picture, a different result. We can learn a great deal from this example, as we adults will need to use mental pictures as part of the process of reprogramming our subconscious minds.

Much of our lives are led in the subconscious, as much of what we do is subconsciously controlled. I like to use the example of the first time you drove a car. Do you remember how difficult it was to consciously remember everything you must do? The conscious mind can only do a few things at the same time. Now that you have driven for several years, you do it subconsciously. You can be listening to the radio, talking on your cell phone, or doing many other things consciously without thinking about driving the car. Your subconscious drives it for you with very little help from your conscious mind.

While people who drive to the same place to work every day had to follow directions to get their initially, they soon turn the task over to their subconscious. Once in a while they have to go somewhere other than work in the morning, but find themselves subconsciously heading toward their place of business. They have to turn around and go in the right direction, because the subconscious minds were taking them away from where they needed to be. Their subconscious minds were taking them away from where they needed to be.

Herein lies the problem. Many of the habits we have programmed into our subconscious serve us well, but there are others that take us away from where we really want to be. Also, most of us have a need for additional positive habits that need to be developed to take us toward the important goals in our lives.

Did you ever play golf with someone who was playing for the first time? He had taken some lessons and his golf instructor had taught him some important components of the golf swing. He needs to keep his left arm straight, keep his head still, twist his body a certain way, keep his head down, follow through on the swing, etc. Now when he is out on the golf course for the first time, he stands over the ball for an eternity trying to remember everything he was taught. The problem is the conscious mind cannot do all those things at the same time.

The golf professional doesn't take all day before hitting the ball. He has programmed his swing one aspect at a time, through practice and repetition, until he does everything necessary to correctly hit the ball. If his game isn't going well, he may work on one aspect of his swing, but he certainly is not trying to consciously remember every component of the process. When he is playing, his conscious mind is focusing on strategy, wind direction, or course layout; the golf swing is already programmed. In reality, Tiger Woods is winning millions of dollars every year by playing golf subconsciously.

Your subconscious mind is your best friend. You think your dog is your best friend? No way. You think your spouse is your best friend? Huh-uh. You think your best friend is your best friend? Afraid not. Your subconscious mind will do everything in its power to do what it believes you want it to do. It is totally focused on serving you, and nothing else matters. The best part is that it serves you twenty-four hours a day, seven days a week, fifty-two weeks a year. It is indefatigable; it never tires.

The best part of having your subconscious be totally dedicated to you is that it is extremely powerful. Let me give you an amazing example. The process of hypnotism is a little frightening to some people. It shouldn't be, as it is really just a process of a hypnotist taking one through a procedure that allows him to talk directly to the subject's subconscious, while the conscious mind remains in the background. Because of the awesome power of the subconscious, much can be accomplished. If a person were hypnotized and then told that a burning cigarette was a pencil, the hypnotist could touch the subject on the bare arm with the hot end without the subject experiencing any pain. In addition, there will be no burn blister! If on the other hand, the hypnotist touched him with a pencil, and told him it was a hot cigarette, the subject would scream in pain. The most amazing part is that, shortly thereafter, a burn blister would appear! No wonder the placebo effect has been used so successfully in the past. If you believe something, and your subconscious embraces that belief, then it is true for you.

I am suggesting that you reprogram your subconscious mind to ensure that you are opening yourself up to the information you need to accomplish the important goals in your life. Also, this reprogramming will cause you to automatically do all the correct things you need to do to accomplish those goals. Imagine that. Not only would you be consciously receiving all the necessary information for success, but your subconscious actions also would be the exact behavior needed to take you there. What a powerful combination.

Take a look at this podium which I am standing behind. Before it ever was a podium, someone had to create it in his mind; then draw a picture of it, probably a blueprint; and finally, build it. It, like everything else, was created mentally before it came to fruition in the physical world. Every table in this room was created mentally before it became a table; every light bulb, every article of clothing, every car, every house, every company was created mentally before they can become physical entities. So understanding all of this, I am suggesting that you mentally create your future, the future you have always wanted, and then reprogram your subconscious mind to ensure that it comes to be.

So now let's discuss exactly how we go about the reprogramming process. I'll bet many of you think that the process of readjusting your subconscious is going to be a difficult undertaking, but fortunately, just the opposite is true. The process is easy, because you've been doing it your whole life. You have been directing your subconscious mind every day through your self- talk. By using this internal dialogue, you program what you believe, how you react, what you consciously hear, and so many other aspects of who you are. Yes, the internal dialogue is a mechanism you used to create and re-create yourself. Now you need to use it on purpose and with a purpose.

Start creating a picture of who you want to be and what you want to accomplish, and communicate those visions to your subconscious mind. Once it embraces and believes these visions, it will begin to let in information you need to bring them to fruition. It will also start the process of creating positive habit patterns that are necessary to the accomplishment of your desired outcome. The vehicle you use to securely implant those visions is affirmations.

Beginning a program of regular affirmations, if done properly, will quickly and effectively reprogram your subconscious mind to where you need to be. Once it is reprogrammed, you will experience your life moving rapidly forward toward your designated destination. If you don't participate in this process correctly, however, nothing will change and you will quickly discontinue the program. There are eight rules to this process, and each rule is critical to its success.

Rule #1 *An affirmation is merely a statement you make to yourself out loud. It must be short—one or two sentences.*

Rule #2 *Write all the affirmations on index cards, so you are always affirming exactly the same words.*

Rule #3 *Say each affirmation at least twice a day.*

Rule #4 *Each affirmation must be in the now—the present tense. You state the affirmation as if it has already happened.*

Rule #5 *As you are saying the words, vividly picture what you are affirming.* Remember, pictures have a powerful impact on the subconscious.

Rule #6 *Inject a feeling of emotion into the pictures.*

Rule #7 *As you are engaged in this program, be very careful of your self-talk. All day, every day, you are communicating with yourself; so be sure the communication is posi-*

tive and doesn't contradict your affirmations. This is, perhaps, the most difficult part of the process. We are all in the habit of speaking to ourselves in a certain way, with a certain tone. By being more conscious of what we are continually saying to ourselves and then adjusting that dialogue, we make the entire affirmation process possible. Leave out this part of the equation and you might as well abandon the entire program.

Rule #8 *Do not use negative affirmations introduced by "don't" or "I won't."* Remember, a negative picture is a negative picture and will produce negative results—like "don't run."

I now will make a prediction. Those of you who immediately start this program will all have the same thought cross your minds two weeks from now—Zors is completely crazy. Yes, after two weeks you will probably experience nothing special. You see, it takes a while for your subconscious to embrace and believe what you are affirming. Don't give up after two weeks; keep at it, and shortly thereafter you will begin to experience some interesting results.

The first thing you will notice is that you will begin to be exposed to information that is connected to what you are affirming. Most people initially believe that this is a coincidence, but soon realized that the process is working. Soon thereafter, you will begin to realize a change in your habit patterns. Now you are really rolling, but the best part, the magical part, is about to begin and really rock your world.

Let's use the example of an overweight man who wants to use affirmations to lose weight. He weighs 200 pounds and affirms, "I can lose 25 pounds."

His subconscious responds, "Yes, you can lose 25 pounds, but you probably won't."

After a while, this gentleman gets smart and starts to affirm, "I weigh 175 pounds" (even though he really weighs 200 pounds).

His subconscious responds, "No, you weigh 200 pounds."

Once again he affirms, "I weigh 175 pounds."

Again his subconscious responds, "You weigh 200 pounds. What's the matter, weren't you listening?"

"I weigh 175 pounds."

"You weigh 200 pounds, so please quit arguing."

"I weigh 175 pounds"

Anyway, after numerous affirmations, the subconscious relents and concludes that this man must weigh 175 pounds. The subconscious begins to let in information through the internal receiver about how to lose weight, and begins the process of changing habit patterns . A week later the man weighs 197 pounds and is going in the right direction, but not fast enough. Since he is still affirming that he already weighs 175 pounds, the subconscious becomes stressed and begins to panic. In its panic it seeks out its friend, the creative subconscious, and asks for its help. Once the creative subconscious joins in the process, the magic begins. This is when the use of the brain goes from 10% to 12%, 15%, 20% and beyond.

The creative subconscious has access to all the information this gentleman has ever been exposed to. Everything he has ever seen, felt, smelled, heard, or tasted is available to it. Even though most of this information has been blocked from his conscious mind, all of it has been stored in his subconscious. The volume of this information dwarfs the data that is presently being shown to the man by his internal receiver. If the man is 40 years old, he has 40 years of information stored in his subconscious—every piece of information he has ever been exposed to. The creative subconscious has access to all of it.

In addition to this vast library of information, the creative subconscious has another powerful advantage. It knows everything about this guy. It knows his physical makeup, his mindset, his strengths and weaknesses—everything there is to know about him. With all of this information at his disposal, the creative subconscious puts together a tailor-made program for our pudgy friend. It is the absolute perfect weight- loss program specifically for him. Remember, he is now using a much greater percentage of his brain, so special results will occur.

Now it gets a little scary. The subconscious will feed this program to the conscious mind in one of two ways. Sometimes it unveils this perfect plan a little at a time, but more often than not, it releases the entire program all at one time.

The first time someone stresses his subconscious to the point where it engages the creative subconscious, a special part of the person's mind is being used for the first time. Since this phenomenon is new, the unveiling of that perfect plan is unsettling. The person often doesn't really understand that this plan is coming from his own mind. People sometimes believe that some "outside force" has given them the information. It is not an outside force, it is the creative subconscious, so don't overreact. When this occurs, you are accessing a wonderful mechanism that you can use the rest of your life. It can give you a tremendous competitive edge, as most people never stress their subconscious to the point where they access their creative subconscious.

All of us know people who are leaders—people we look up to and respect. Often, while we want to be that kind of person, we don't believe we can. "Why, I am just me," we say to ourselves. Well you know, you are correct, you are just you—but you are just you who has a fantastic mind. Now you have a tool to enable you to use a much greater percentage of that mind. There is no excuse for you not to be able to accomplish anything in life that you desire.

Do you want to run a highly successful company? Create the picture in your mind, start the affirmation process to program your subconscious, and just do it.

Do you want to be the leader of the community? Just do it. You want to be a great husband or a great wife? Just do it. Do you want to be a great Sunday school teacher? Just do it!

As you do all these things and more, as they come to fruition, you automatically become a person of internal locus of control. You will no longer be a person of external control, who is like a leaf on a tree. When the leaf finally falls from the tree, it goes where the wind wants it to go; it has no say of its own.

A person of internal locus of control, however, is like a thoroughbred horse in the starting gate—he knows where the finish line is, and he knows he can get there, and get there first. So with this in mind, my friends, I want to challenge all of you with the words of the songwriter Dan Fogelberg:

And it is run for the roses
As fast as you can
Your fate is delivered
Your moment's at hand
It's a chance of a lifetime,
In a lifetime of chance
And it's high time you joined in the dance
It's high time you joined in the dance.

—

Zors: Does anyone have any questions?

Question: I am continually engaged in some type of program or process to become more productive, happier or more successful. All these systemized ap-

proaches have been fruitful, but sometimes I feel stuck. How do I make sure I am always growing?

Zors: To grow as a person, in my opinion, involves three behaviors. The first of two I learned from Charlie "Tremendous" Jones, who tells us that we all will be the same in five years as we are today, except for the books we read and the people we meet. He is correct, so we need to choose our books and associates wisely. The third behavior has to do with personal courage. If we are to experience real growth, we need to venture out of our comfort zones. As long as we stay buttoned up in a comfort zone, we are stuck. Getting out of that zone and moving into somewhere that is not comfortable regenerates the growing process. After a while the non-comfort zone becomes comfortable, which tells us that growth has taken place. It also tells us that it is time to venture out again.

There is another important point I need to make here, and it is important. Taking yourself out of your comfort zone does not mean abandoning those things that are working for you. Sometimes people get bored with their success, so they make changes for the sake of variety and excitement. This is really quite foolish, as it is the same as turning your back on success.

Question: I have noticed that you have a set formula on how to live and how to succeed. I know several very successful, happy people who do not em-

brace any of your techniques. What makes you think your way is the only way?

Zors: I don't believe I ever said that my way is the only way. At least I hope not, as that would not be true. I know there are many roads to the top of the mountain. I also know there is a huge library of information out there on how one can improve his or her life. Much of this information is excellent, and some is not. The philosophy I profess, on a regular basis, works. I know because it has worked for me and many of my associates. If someone has another method of accomplishing what he needs to accomplish, that is great. I, however, am limited to sharing what I know really works.

Question: When a ninety-five percenter is exposed to some of these dynamic ideas, how can he justify not at least giving some a try?

Zors: During the Katrina floods, a minister found himself trapped in his house. The water was up to the top of his front steps, when a man in a boat came by and offered to take him to safety. "I'll be okay for a while," he said "I have prayed and God will take care of me. Go save those who are more in need."

Several hours later, he was forced to go up to the second floor of his house. The floodwaters had engulfed his entire downstairs. As he looked out of his upstairs window, he saw another boat approaching. Again he refused his opportunity to be taken to safety, as he again told the rescuer that he had prayed and

God would take care of him, so the person should help others more in need.

A few hours later the man had moved up to his roof and the water was up to his waist. Just then a helicopter hovered over him with a rope ladder hanging down to allow him to climb to safety. The minister, for the third time, refused help and began to pray again.

Shortly thereafter, the minister opened his eyes to discover that he was with God in Heaven. He had died. "God," he said, "I prayed and prayed. Why didn't you save me?"

With that God replied, "What are you talking about? I sent you two boats and a helicopter!"

You see, when you share dynamic information with someone, it is up to him or her as to whether to use it or not. I don't know why, but many people just find it very difficult to make necessary changes in their lives. They find it far less threatening to just ignore life-changing advice.

4
Convincing Others

Good evening. I am happy to be here tonight and anxious to share some ideas with all of you. I feel especially energetic this evening because I was able to win an argument with Ruth earlier today. I convinced her to compromise. You see, for me, getting her to compromise is like winning, because with her, that is about the best I can do. The discussion centered on her desire to buy an expensive new coat. I told her that I had budgeted for a new car, so the coat was out of the question. Finally we compromised. We got her a new coat, but we keep it in the garage.

In our quest for accomplishment, it is often important to convince others to agree with our way of thinking. This can be especially difficult when it requires others to change their thinking, or perhaps even their future action. Our inability to get others to change their minds can be a serious impediment to reaching our goals. It can also cause one to have a new coat and an old car in his garage!

Earlier in my career I came to the realization that my ability to bring people around to my way of thinking was critical in my quest for success. With this in mind, I began a serious program of research into the science of salesmanship. What were the methods successful salespeople use to convince others to think a certain way or to take a desired action?

I am sure you know that there is a mountain of information on how to sell. Like everything else in life, some of this information is excellent and some is not. After years of research and experimentation, I believe I have devised a rather simple formula that one can use to us effectively convince people to consider adjusting their thought process and their subsequent actions. There are four parts to this formula, and I will share them with you now.

The first concept I would like you to consider is something I call *ego control*. This involves controlling our own egos while understanding how powerfully others are controlled by their own egos.

Controlling our egos is not only important to the sales process, but essential in all aspects of life. There've been many people I have known who have gone through life with closed minds, because they believed their way was the only way. There is so much to learn from everyone, so these people miss out and their lives suffer because of their condescending attitude. The first step in controlling our egos is to willfully release the illusion that our way is the only way.

When in a situation where it is important to convince someone to accept your way of thinking, remember that it is never an ego competition. Once someone suspects that his ego is under attack, he will always dig in. That is why arguing with someone seldom works. The reason you are arguing, by the way, is because your own ego is out of control. When in any selling situation, leave your ego at the door and allow the other person's ego to feel safe. You can complement someone's way of thinking while gently exposing your own concept. Remember to not win the battle of words while badly losing the war.

The second critical piece to the sales formula is credibility. I will not go into a lot of detail about this now, as I will be talking about this at our next meeting. I would like to create a scenario, however, to demonstrate how important credibility is in the sales process.

The quintessential sales situation is the job interview. In that setting an individual is attempting to sell an interviewer the merits of hiring him, so in reality, he is selling himself. Now let's say that you are a chief marketing officer at a company who is looking to hire a sales manager, and I am a candidate for that job. I have a 10 o'clock appointment to be interviewed by you, so I am in the lobby of your company at nine fifty-five. At that time you are completing a telephone conversation with a friend of yours. This friend, by the way, is someone you have known for many years and completely trust.

"I have to go now," you say. "I have a gentleman in the lobby waiting to be interviewed for our sales manager's job."

"Who will you be interviewing?" Your friend asks.

"A guy named Michael Zors. Do you know him?"

"Yes, I know him," he replies. "And I believe you are wasting your time. Michael Zors is not someone you want to hire. He will say whatever is convenient, has a terrible work ethic, and is not at all that smart."

Since your friend is someone whose judgment you totally respect, I now have a problem. If you still give me the courtesy of an interview, I am not going to get that job. It doesn't matter how effectively I answer your questions, or how impressive my resume is; I am not credible in your eyes. The fact that I have no credibility in this situation prevents me from having any chance.

If, on the other hand, your friend had said, "Do yourself a favor and hire him on the spot, before someone else does. He is the most effective business person I've ever known, and will make you look like a genius if he comes to work for you."

Now the interview will take on a completely different tone. Even if I am not at my very best in the interview, I would still have an excellent chance of getting that job. Because of your trusted friend, I would have instant credibility with you, which is critical in the interview process.

Think about it—if you don't trust someone, what are the chances you will be convinced by that person to do anything? The sales process comes to a screeching halt when it is determined that the seller is not to be trusted or believed. That is why it is so important to develop credibility with anyone you wish to convince of anything. At our next meeting, I will discuss that concept and a powerful way you can create outstanding credibility.

The third ingredient in convincing someone to accept your way of thinking is preparation. If you are totally prepared to respond effectively to whatever question or comment surfaces in a selling situation, you're on your way to a successful conclusion. Let me explain by using the same example of a job interview.

A friend of yours has told you about an open executive position with his company, and he has set up an interview for you with the decision-maker for a week from now. Obviously he has spoken well of you to the interviewer, which will help with your credibility, but he has done something even more helpful. Since he knows that the interview will be key to getting you hired, he has prepared you for that meeting in a unique way. He knows the decision-maker is going to ask you twelve specific questions during the interview, and your responses will be extremely important in the evaluation process. For this reason your friend secretly gives you a list of what those twelve questions will be. This gives you a week to prepare perfect answers to those questions. Can you imagine what an advantage you have over all the other applicants?

You don't need a friend to give you an advanced list of questions. You can figure them out for yourself. If you mentally put yourself in the place of the interviewer, you can create a list of every possible question. I know people who have done this, and they tell me there are only about one hundred possible questions one can ask in an interview for any job. You could create that list and the corresponding best answers. While this is time-consuming, it is certainly worth the effort. You then spend the time necessary to totally familiarize yourself with those answers.

One friend used to practice this process while driving to and from work, and it took about one month for him to be proficient at answering all the questions. When he began the actual interview process, he got six job offers from six interviews. He was 6 for 6 because he was so much more impressive in the interviews than the other applicants. You see, most people are not prepared for a job interview; in fact, most people are not prepared for most selling situations.

In any situation where you need to convince someone of anything, be prepared. There are only so many questions or objections you will need to counter, so if you have anticipated what they will be, your preparation will enable you to overcome any hurdles you might encounter.

The final and most important piece in the sales process is to inject emotion into the process. People generally believe that if they can successfully demonstrate the logic of making a change, they can convince another to make that change. You see, all true sales are really the act of convincing someone to make some kind of change. In most cases, however, most people are not moved toward change because of logic; they are convinced to take action because of emotion. They do use logic, however, to justify that emotional decision.

The car salesman doesn't make the sale because the buyer sees the logic in purchasing a certain car. The sale is made because that new car appeals to the buyer on an emotional level. That car announces to the world something about the driver. Since the car is often an extension of the buyer's ego, the sales process includes both emotion and ego. Obviously, preparation and credibility play a role as well.

When you are in a situation where you need to cause someone to change his way of thinking and accept yours, you need to use all four parts of the formula to increase your chances of success. You must have credibility, be prepared to respond to all questions and objections, use powerful emotion, and be extremely aware of both his and your egos. Remember that there can be more than one correct action in dealing with any situation so you need to use all four of these tools to get agreement that your recommended action is the correct choice.

—

Zors: Are there any questions?

Question: I am having trouble understanding how to inject emotion into the sales process. Can you give me an example?

Zors: There are two good methods to do this. One is to discover the subject's dissatisfaction with his status quo, and then show him how the change you are suggesting will eliminate that dissatisfaction. The other is to demonstrate how changing to what you are proposing will positively stroke his ego.

Question: I'm sorry, that answer didn't help me at all. I have no idea what you mean.

Zors: Okay, let me be more specific. Let's say that you work for one of many companies that performs lawn care service. You know, they come out once a week to fertilize and spray for weeds. You are trying to get me to change from my present service to yours. You need to find out what I don't like about my present service. If you ask me if I like my present service or not, you won't get the information you need. Since I chose this service, I am not going to tell you that I am dissatisfied. My ego doesn't want you to know that I made a bad decision.

If, however, you praise me for picking such a fine company, but then ask, "If you could change one thing about your present lawn care company, what would it be?" Then, sure that my ego is safe, I would tell you what I don't like about my service. You would then show me how your service wouldn't cause me any such problems.

The other way is to convince me that your services will make my lawn looks so much better than it does now, the rest of the neighborhood will be in awe. This will appeal to my ego.

The Race

Whenever I start to hang my head in front of failure's face,
my downward fall is broken by the memory of a race.
A children's race, young boys, young men; how I remember well,
excitement sure, but also fear, it wasn't hard to tell.
They all lined up so full of hope, each thought to win that race
or tie for first, or if not that, at least take second place.
Their parents watched from off the side, each cheering for their son,
and each boy hoped to show his folks that he would be the one.

The whistle blew and off they flew, like chariots of fire,
to win, or be the hero there, was each young boy's desire.
One boy in particular, whose dad was in the crowd,
was running in the lead and thought, "My dad would be so proud."
But as he speeded down the field and crossed a shallow dip,
the little boy who thought he'd win, lost his step and slipped.
Trying hard to catch himself, his arms flew every place,
And midst the laughter of the crowd he fell flat on his face.
As he fell, his hope fell too; he couldn't win it now.
Humiliated, he just wished to disappear somehow.

But as he fell his dad stood up and showed his anxious face,
which to the boy so clearly said, "Get up and win that race!"
He quickly rose, no damage done, behind a bit that's all,

and ran with all his mind and might to make up for his fall.
So anxious to restore himself, to catch up and to win, his mind went faster than his legs. He slipped and fell again.
He wished that he had quit before with only one disgrace.
"I'm hopeless as a runner now, I shouldn't try to race."

But through the laughing crowd he searched and found his father's face
with a steady look that said again, "Get up and win that race!"
So he jumped up to try again, ten yards behind the last.
"If I'm to gain those yards," he thought, "I've got to run real fast!"
Exceeding everything he had, he regained eight, then ten…
But trying hard to catch the lead, he slipped and fell again.
Defeat! He lay there silently. A tear dropped from his eye.
"There's no sense running anymore! Three strikes I'm out! Why try?
I've lost, so what's the use?" he thought. "I'll live with my disgrace."
But then he thought about his dad, who soon he'd have to face.

"Get up," an echo sounded low, "you haven't lost at all,
for all you have to do to win is rise each time you fall.
Get up!" The echo urged him on, "get up and take your place!
You were not meant for failure here! Get up and win that race!"
So, up he rose to run once more, refusing to forfeit, and he resolved that win or lose, at least he wouldn't quit.

So far behind the others now, the most he'd ever been,
still he gave it all he had and ran like he could win.
Three times he'd fallen stumbling, three times he rose again.
Too far behind to hope to win, he still ran to the end.

They cheered another boy who crossed the line and won first place,
head high and proud and happy—no falling, no disgrace.
But, when the fallen youngster crossed the line, in last place,
the crowd gave him a greater cheer for finishing the race.
And even though he came in last with head bowed low, un-proud,
you would have thought he'd won the race, to listen to that crowd.
And to his dad he sadly said, "I didn't do so well."
"To me, you won," his father said. "You rose each time you fell."

And now when things seem dark and bleak and difficult to face,
the memory of that little boy helps me in my own race.
For all of life is like that race, with ups and downs and all.
And all you have to do to win is rise each time you fall.
And when depression and despair shout loudly in my face,
another voice within me says, "Get up and win that race!"

–Attributed to D. H. Groberg–

5

The Power of Commitment

Good evening. It is wonderful to be here tonight to have an opportunity to share some ideas with all of you. It is interesting to note that we have a standing room only crowd here tonight, and yet everyone arrived early. I know that some of you really enjoy these monthly get-togethers and don't want to miss anything, but I don't believe that is entirely the reason for such punctuality.

Those of you who have been coming to these talks regularly, and those of you who know me, also know that I am always on time to start the program on time. Isn't it interesting to realize that the way you perceive me affects your reaction to me? While some may believe that being unpredictable is a positive attribute, there is certainly something to be said for projecting an image of consistency. Emerson said that a foolish consistency is the hobgoblin of little minds, but there are some consistencies that really are not foolish at all.

The way others perceive you has a powerful impact on your effectiveness in dealing with them. Those things that you do on a consistent basis paint a picture of who you are to the world. If I were one who didn't respect your time and sometimes started these meetings later than announced, I am sure people would be wandering in at all different times. My consistency in starting promptly, however, painted a picture of me and cause all of you to react a certain way.

Who you are is important. It causes you to do what you do and makes others react to you in a certain way. We all have a vision of ourselves and generally are true to that vision. For this reason we should work diligently to create a self vision of who we want and need to be, and then be consistently true to that image. That consistency is the projection by which we present ourselves to the world.

I believe Emerson was describing our thought processes when he coined his now famous phrase. If we have a consistent belief in something that is wrong, then our stubbornness traps us in a place where we shouldn't be. Highly successful people have the ability to willfully release illusion, and then are very careful to fill that void with something significant.

If I wish to project an image of myself as an honest, reliable, affable, intelligent, caring person; I have to consistently be that person. The hardest part of projecting an image of what we want others to see is to become that image—that person. We can't project who we aren't, so let's talk about creating and projecting that quintessential image.

I know that many of you have great respect for the concept of commitment. If you make a commitment to someone, you try to keep it. You know, though, what Yoda said about try. I agree with him when he says, "Try not. Do or do not. There is no try."

Keeping commitments is a critical ingredient in your credibility, and your credibility is so very essential in the image you need to project. When you commit to something, move heaven and earth to keep it. No matter how small, every commitment is important because you are forming a powerful habit.

Be consistent in keeping your word. If you tell someone that you will call him tomorrow, call him tomorrow. If you tell someone you will meet him at noon for lunch be there at noon. When you say something, others should know that it is always valid. When I say these meetings will start at seven o'clock, that doesn't mean 7:01. My reputation is important to me, so I need for people to know that every commitment, no matter how small, is of utmost importance.

Another important point—do not commit to something you do not control. It is better to tell someone that you will do everything in your power to get something done, than to commit and have someone else's inabilities cause you not to keep a commitment. Everyone with whom you come in contact is formulating an opinion of you. If you aren't reliable, you send a strong negative message to everyone you know.

I am fortunate enough to know many of you personally, and I believe that most of you take your commitments seriously. I am suggesting, however, that you take your commitments very seriously. Doing so will have a dynamic, positive impact on all of your relationships.

I know that is easy for you to understand why this behavior so important. There is another kind of commitment, however, that is even more important. These are commitments we make to ourselves.

Sometimes it isn't too difficult to break little promises to others, especially if they are close friends or family. These, of course, are the very people we should never let down. The most important pledges we must keep, however, are the ones we make to ourselves. Unfortunately, these are the very easiest to break; after all, we can always rationalize that kind of behavior, as we will not hold a grudge against ourselves. At the same time, however, doing so will damage our self-trust.

If we do not take the commitments we make to ourselves seriously, we consistently undermine the process of creating an inward trust. Without it, it doesn't make much sense for us to establish personal goals. I often preach about how important it is to establish goals for oneself; but frankly, it's a waste of time if you are not true to self-commitment. The biggest reason people do not succeed is that they do not establish goals; the second biggest is they do not keep their commitments necessary in reaching these goals. Commitment to oneself is paramount in accomplishing outstanding achievements. For that very reason, we must get into the habit of keeping all promises, big or small, we make to ourselves.

How many times do people pledge to lose weight, quit smoking, get in shape, clean the garage, or dozens of other little commitments? How many times do they rationalize not getting these things done? Every time you commit to accomplishing something and then find an excuse for not keeping that commitment, you weaken your self-credibility—and let's face it, if you can't trust yourself, who can you trust?

I am suggesting that you stop making any pledge to yourself unless you hold that pledge sacred. When you do make a self-commitment, whether it is big or small, be sure to see it through to fruition. With this process you begin to form the habit of keeping your word to yourself. When even the smallest commitment is held dear, you send a powerful message to your subconscious mind. Soon you will form the habit of always being true to yourself. Once you do this, you unleash one of the most powerful tools available to you.

Remember, all kept commitments, internal or external, large or small, personal or professional, contribute to an ongoing announcement to the world that you are one to be trusted and one who gets things done.

Zors: Are there any questions?

Question: I have always learned to state my self-commitments out loud to others to lock myself in the keeping these commitments. This seems to work for me. What do you think of that idea?

Zors: It's a good idea, and I would think it is effective. There are certain promises you make to yourself that you do not wish to share, though. If you are in the habit of keeping all commitments you make to yourself, it is never necessary to publicly state your intentions.

Question: If your son were leaving home to go out into the world to make his fortune, and you could give him only three pieces of advice, what would they be?

Zors: Listen to daddy, listen to daddy, listen to daddy.

But seriously, if I had a son and he was about to make his way in the world, he wouldn't need advice at that point in his life. If I had done my job as a father, I would have already sown all the seeds necessary for him to do what he must do and be who we must be. I would not be so naïve as to believe he had embraced all my advice at that time, but he would have the seeds, which would soon be cultivated by life's experience.

I think you are really asking me to give you three powerful pieces of advice to apply to your own life or to share with your children. I will be glad to do that.

The three most important concepts I can share with you tonight, not necessarily in priority order, are:

- Remember that you create your own life mentally, before it manifests itself in the physical plane.
- Remember that if you are not in the habit of keeping in the commitments you make to yourself, your goal setting activity is a waste of time.
- Be careful what you project out into the world, as it will surely be returned to you.

Question: Can you recommend some books that could help us expand our knowledge of success techniques?

Zors: Sure, but remember, just knowing something is pretty useless unless you are applying that knowledge on a consistent basis. There are a lot of wonderful books I can recommend to you. Here are just a few:

- *Think and Grow Rich*
- *Raving Fans*
- *The Bible*
- *The Autobiography of Benjamin Franklin*
- *The Parable of the Homemade Millionaire*
- *The Master Key System*
- *How to Win Friends and Influence People*
- *The Power of Positive Thinking*
- *Life Is Tremendous*

6
Little Things Mean a Lot

Good evening. It is great to be here tonight to share some ideas with you. I hope you didn't come here expecting to hear something big. I have a fascination with little things in life, and that is what I want to discuss with you.

I know that it is important to think big and have giant expectations in our lives, but it is often those little details that get us there. Consistently doing the important little things throughout our lives can magnify into something very big over time. If, for instance, a twenty-year-old started saving just ten dollars a day and continued that process until age 65, with compound interest, he would have over $800,000 for retirement. You see, it is the consistency over time that make something very insignificant grow to something quite significant.

On the other hand, consistently committing small errors, intensified over time, can completely undermine one's ambition. Let's say that you had a weapon that shoots a very powerful laser and wanted to use it to kill a dangerous man-eating lion hundred feet away from you. You aim the laser at the lion's heart, but when you pull the trigger you miss his heart by one inch. Chances are pretty good that you would still kill the beast. If the lion were a mile away, however, that faulty aim, which was off by 1 inch at 100 feet, at one-mile would miss the lion by 44 feet! So remember, a small error multiplied by time or distance, can grow to be a giant problem.

Let's use Kevin Sutherland as an example. Kevin is a professional golfer who won $751,626 on the Professional Golfers Association tour in 2006. Obviously this is a good living, even though he has a lot of expenses that come out of those earnings. The leading money winner that same year was Tiger Woods. In 2006 he won $9,941,563 in tour events. That is more than thirteen times the winnings enjoyed by Kevin Sutherland.

It appears obvious that Tiger Woods is a much better golfer than Kevin Sutherland. How much better? Fewer than one stroke per nine holes of golf! Tiger averaged 68.79 strokes per eighteen holes of golf, while Kevin averaged 70.56. That small difference enabled Tiger to earn nine million dollars more than Kevin, a huge payoff for a small difference. Now you know why professional golfers are so punctilious with each shot.

If you will actively endeavor to form habit patterns that ensure the constant correct completion of little tasks, the process will reward you in a big way. A great way to evaluate the process that is unique to you is to analyze exactly how you utilize your time. We all have 24 hours a day, so it is our ability to get the most out of those 24 hours that will set us apart from everyone else. Please note that I am not saying that it is important to work more hours than everyone else; I am talking about utilizing our time to our maximum advantage.

Tonight I am going to be suggesting several activities you may wish to become involved in which will catapult you over and above your competition in achieving success. All of these activities, while they may seem small and insignificant on the surface, are very effective in making a positive difference in your quest to separate yourself from the pack. Your initial thought, however, will be that you do not have enough time to do most of them. That is why it is imperative to analyze and understand the process of maximizing your available time.

The first step is to eliminate the negative habits you have formed that steal your time, and then replace them with habits that help you become highly organized. In your analyzation process, you will become aware of how much work you do that has absolutely no impact on anything important. This is just busy work that allows you to do what you like to do, rather than what you need to do. Busy work is like treading water, it gets you no closer to your goals. By creating a "must do" list each day that has your highest priorities first and the lesser priorities near the bottom, you can stay on track. Just discipline yourself to complete the highest priority on the sheet before going on to the next priority.

Another great time waster occurs when you try to work too fast and, in doing so, you commit errors. Obviously, having to undo an error and start over is a huge drain on one's time. That is why it is not always wise to practice multi-tasking, because you are not totally focused on any single task.

The point of all this is that if you properly organize your life, you have more than enough time to get done what you need to get done, and have time left over just for fun. I sincerely believe this, and that is why I am sure you will have the time to inject some of my "small things" behavior into your life.

The first suggestion I will submit is for you to become more informed each day. We are always learning through life experiences, but if you want to learn at a faster pace than your peers, you need to begin a specific program to enhance your knowledge.

Many years ago I was fortunate enough to hear a great speaker comment on the subject of becoming more informed. Earl Nightingale spoke of using one hour per day to study about the field in which you are presently engaged. This is above and beyond learning through on-the-job training. He went on to say that, after a few years, all that additional knowledge will surely make you an expert in your field, and experts are always pursued by their industry.

If you will get into the habit of studying for one hour per day, you will immediately put yourself on a lifelong program of self-improvement. In addition, it will separate you from the masses, as most will not discipline themselves to do this. There is, by the way, a method of manufacturing an hour per day to use for this endeavor. It is a concept used by brilliant people to create time for their academic enlightenment. The concept is based on the utilization of found time.

How many times do you find yourself sitting somewhere, waiting for someone, completely bored? We have all had the experience of being in a waiting room or lobby waiting for a doctor, lawyer, business person, or almost anyone. Often you fill that time by reading some magazine that is stacked on the table next to you. Most of the time the information in that magazine is of no real interest or help to you. It certainly has nothing to do with your goals and priorities.

What if, during these wasted times, you were prepared with a book or article you wanted and needed to read? If, at every opportunity, you used these found time intervals to help complete your hour per day study commitment, you would realize it is quite easy to complete that task each day. Turning wasted time in the found time is a powerful concept used by the most intelligent among us.

The next suggestion is one that people do not want to hear or do. For a variety of reasons, however, it is as important as anything else in life. Find the time to exercise one hour per day. The excuse is always, "I don't have the time," but that is just poppycock. I'll bet all of you watch television for at least an hour a day; if you really want to multi-task, then exercise while you're watching your favorite shows.

I don't care what exercise program you commit to, as long as you research it and utilize it correctly and safely. Also, it is important to get your doctor's okay before starting. Here are the reasons this is so very important:

- Do it for your health. You can't be successful if you are sick all the time, nor can you enjoy the success you achieve.
- Do it to increase your energy level.
- Do it to look healthy and successful.
- Do it to burn up stress. This is essential in helping you become who you want to become.

Remember, highly successful people are often those who are healthy, look good, have an abundance of energy, and are in control of their stress levels. Consistent, effective exercise can help put you in that group.

This next suggestion will not seem like a big deal, but it really is. It is important to thank people.

We live in a relationship world, and building and retaining relationships is not only critical to our success, but is essential to our enjoyment of life. We must treat others well if we are to enjoy numerous and long-lasting relationships. Saying a meaningful thank you is so important and so easy to do! Equally important is to look for excuses to send thank you notes or emails to people. They're always appreciated, and the practice keeps you connected with the rest of the world.

My next suggestion is to return every phone call on the same day you receive it. It doesn't matter if you want to talk to the person or not—get in the habit of doing this. Think of how you feel if someone doesn't return your call, or takes days to call you back. It makes you believe that the other person doesn't think you are very important, which is a real slap in the face. If that is how you feel, don't do it to anyone else. Returning telephone calls promptly has the reverse effect, and will pay huge dividends toward maintaining relationships.

Returning phone calls brings up another important point. Don't do to other people the things that annoy you. Did you ever get a voicemail message in which the caller wants you to call him back, but he rattles the number off so quickly you have to listen to the voice mail several times to extract the correct number? If you hate that, don't do it to anyone else. Think about all the little things in life that others do to annoy you, and then make sure you don't do them to others.

Another small act that pays big dividends is using names. Nothing is more flattering or personal than hearing someone use your name. If, however, you overdo this while conversing with someone, it sounds fake and destroys the effort. A great rule of thumb is to say the person's name at the beginning of the conversation, once in the middle, and at the conclusion.

Next suggestion—pay yourself first. One of the big problems for most ninety-five percenters is that they, on a regular basis, spend what they earn. We all know that this doesn't work because, in the long run, we are bound to encounter financial emergencies sooner or later. There is a financial plan that I would like to submit to you which, if undertaken, will have multiple benefits for you.

I want you to think about what would happen if your income was suddenly reduced by 5%. This is not something we would want to happen, but really, would your life come to an end? Would you starve? Would you lose your house, your way of life?

I believe that if you had to exist on 5% fewer dollars, you would make changes in your expenditures and get along just fine. We all want more money, but less won't destroy us. That is why I am suggesting that you give away 5 percent of your income on a regular basis. I want all of you to put 5% of what you make into someone else's account. That someone else is the person you are going to be and, since you are not that person yet, the money would no longer belong to the present you.

The account you would set up would be for the future you, for when you retire, and it must be separate from any other retirement accounts you already have. Since this money isn't yours, it is untouchable except in two circumstances. The money will be accessed by the future you upon retirement, but can be borrowed any time before then for emergencies—real emergencies. If you borrow from the account, you must do so with a plan to repay it promptly and with interest. Remember, it is not your money until retirement.

While setting up this account will ensure a better retirement, more importantly, it will establish an emergency fund, which will afford you financial peace of mind. It is too easy to find a way to spend all we earn, but creating this fund causes you to channel these dollars into something important—you are creating wealth.

Well, these are some of the small things that pay off big. I submit to you that small isn't necessarily unimportant. I would rather have a 1 carat diamond than a 100 pound bag of manure.

—

Zors: Are there any questions?

Question: You mentioned wealth in your comments tonight. Why is being rich so important?

Zors: Being rich is important to people who wish to be rich; however, attaining success is different for each person. If you have a worthwhile goal that is important to you and you achieve it, then you are successful. Success isn't measured by what others think; it is measured by your attaining what you truly need in life. Having affluence does, however, afford you a lot of opportunities you may need to accomplish what you want.

Question: How do you feel when people who are exposed to the methodologies you hold dear, don't seem to embrace them?

Zors: What a great question! Thank you. This is something I have had to learn to cope with. It really used to bother me when I shared some technique with someone, a technique I knew worked, only to have them disregarded. I finally figured it out.

There are ninety-five percenters who will always be ninety-five percenters. They are not open to any information that might possibly change their lives. Sometimes this is hard to accept, but that is just the way it is.

There are others, however, who seem to disregard enlightenment, but that isn't really what is happening. When you share something important with them, the idea becomes a seed planted in their consciousness. The seed may never come to fruition, but that is not the norm. Life experiences will often be the catalyst that causes people to embrace those methodologies. Challenges often cause people to become open to new ways to function, and that is one reason challenges are so important in our lives.

Each time you share something significant with another, it has an effect. You may not notice that effect at the time, but something does happen. If you take a rock and hit it with a hammer, you may not notice anything happening. Something does happen, as miniscule cracks are introduced into the rock. The next time you hit the rock, more cracks occur and existing cracks become larger. The effects of the two hits may still be invisible to the naked eye. You hit the rock again and again, and after many strikes, the rock crumbles into little pieces. It appears that the last strike caused this to occur, but it was really the cumulative effect of all the strikes that caused the rock to crumble.

This is exactly what happens when you sow seeds of wisdom—finally, after several strikes, the message enlightens that person to take the desired and necessary action. Remember, you can't jam this information down someone's throat, but you can sow seeds.

Question: Do you have a mentor, and if so, who is he?

Zors: Yes, I do have a mentor who will remain anonymous. It is interesting, however, that you assume my mentor is a man.

The Winds of Fate

One ship drives east and another drives west,
With the self- same winds that blow;
'Tis the set of the sails
And not the gales
That tell them the way to go.

Like the winds of the sea are the winds of fate,
As we voyage along through life,
'Tis a set of the soul
That decides its goal
And not the calm or strife.

—Ella Wheeler Wilcox—

7
Nobility

On this particular evening, since Zors was out of town, Ruth Zors addressed the huge audience who had come to hear him. They were not disappointed.

—

Good evening. It is wonderful to be here tonight to share some ideas with you. For those of you who do not know me, I am Ruth Zors. My husband was called out of town at the last minute, so I will attempt to fill your time with some meaningful concepts.

I am glad that so many of you braved the weather to be here. Like most of you, I am anxious for spring and summer to get here. Zors and I love to picnic at the beach, and I enjoy watching the sailboats. They are particularly beautiful when the sun begins to set.

There is a great lesson to be learned while watching sailboats. As I observe one boat going from west to east, there is another going east to west at the same moment. The fascinating part of this lovely picture is that the two boats that are going in opposite directions are driven by the same wind. The sailors have no control over what the wind will do, but they do control how they will react to whatever nature offers. A good sailor can set his sails to take the ship in whichever direction he wishes. And so it is in life. We are continually subjected to both challenges and blessings that often are not of our doing.

When I was a young girl, I was always struggling with some problem. I remember thinking that if I could eliminate that problem, life would be just great. Eventually the difficulty would go away through one process or another, but a different one would emerge. Again the thought of how wonderful life would be without the new challenge would cross my mind. It took many years, but I finally came to the realization that there will always be challenges, and there was little I could do about it. I could, however, learn how to react to challenges and eliminate them, or use them as a tool for growth.

You see, the world is an equal opportunity challenger. Generally, one person's challenges are no greater than another's. The way one reacts to those challenges, however, can take him in the opposite direction of another.

The manner in which we deal with the positives and negatives, on a daily basis, creates the direction in which our lives will sail. Zors will tell you that challenges are really blessings. When one is in the midst of a serious difficulty, however, that statement is not well received.

Nobility

Rudyard Kipling displays amazing insight when he tells us to meet with Triumph and Disaster and treat those two imposters just the same. The wonderful successes we accomplish and the terrible setbacks we endure are not so intense when we review them a few years later. With the blessing of hindsight, we realize that, generally, these moments were just the normal happenings of life.

Once we form the habit of living life on an even keel, the ups and downs are somewhat neutralized; and while this is quite acceptable to us for the "downs," maybe not so for the "ups". How do we endure such an even-keel existence? Surely we must be allowed to celebrate our victories and curse our defeats. Yes, the even-keel kind of life sounds pretty boring.

I know all of us seek an exciting life, and would not be happy or fulfilled with a vanilla existence. Therefore, I am not suggesting we all schedule a lobotomy as soon as possible. We can, however, lower our excitement when victorious and reduce our depths of despair when defeated, because there is something else we can do to move our lives into a level of positive excitement! That is what I want to share with you this evening.

First of all, it is important to realize that each person on earth has an impact on it. With everything we do, we send out ripples into the sea of humanity. Some ripples are larger and farther reaching than others, but all have an effect. While we are sending out ripples that affect others, we are constantly affected by ripples that are from everyone else. The most powerful ripples are the ones we send out, because they always come back to us. This isn't just my opinion; it has been offered throughout history in many ways.

The religious law that states, "That which you sow, so shall ye reap" is an example of this concept. Another is a scientific law—to every action there is an equal and opposite reaction. Also, how many times have you heard someone say "What goes around comes around?"

There are so many ways that learned people have expressed the concept of a balance in the world that it cannot be denied. You do create your world by what you send out into it. Most of the time there is neither rhyme nor reason to what we radiate, and so what we receive is equally random. It appears that we need a system of ripple sending that is in harmony with the world we wish to create.

You all know that Zors suggests we each have a program of sending out twelve miracles a day. His definition of a miracle is any loving act you do for another. It can he simply opening the door for someone, letting someone in front of you while in traffic, or buying lunch for a friend. It can be more important, like giving your time and resources to a worthwhile cause, or giving blood—the gift of life.

Zors has committed to twelve miracles a day, every day, and it is sometimes humorous to see him work to accomplish that goal. I've seen him writing and sending friendship notes to people at 11 o'clock at night to make sure he gets his twelve miracles in that day. There is an interesting story as to why Zors created the twelve miracles per day program.

Many years ago Zors felt it was important to always be giving more than he received, so he started counting the miracles he gave off, and the miracles he received each day. He wanted to make sure he had a surplus of giving. This program, however, is one of the few major failures Zors has experienced in his life. Day after day he would receive more miracles that he gave. In fact, as he increased his giving, his receiving would increase to a greater degree. That's when he finally changed the program to twelve miracles a day.

You see, it is impossible to give more than you receive. This is true, either way, whether you are giving positives or negatives. Zors often tells us that we own only what we give away. Some don't understand this, so let me try to explain. Please don't tell Zors I said try.

If I give you a beautiful watch as a present, what have I really done? I have given you something that actually isn't real. Only something permanent is real, so the watch doesn't qualify, because it will cease to be at some point in time. And while the watch will become dust someday, I will always have the act of giving it to you. That loving act is good forever, as our souls are forever. Remember, we are not a body that happens to have a soul; we are a soul who happens to have a body.

I would like to take a moment now to clarify something. Many of you who are here tonight have become financially successful by listening to and applying Zors' teachings to your lives. There is absolutely nothing wrong with material success. For one thing, it puts you in a position of strength when enacting miracles. It can help you own your own time. It gives you credibility. How many of you would be here tonight to see and hear Zors if he were on welfare? Make no mistake; I am not minimizing the importance of affluence.

All right, how do we program a process of sending positive ripples, and what do we get out of it? Now please listen to me very carefully. I am going to share something with you that is life-changing. Adopting what I am going to propose will absolutely change the direction of your life, and will take you to another level. I am suggesting that you begin to live life with a noble purpose, and you commit your very existence to that purpose.

I am sure that you have wondered what your purpose is for being here. It is a common question that crosses everyone's mind at some point in his or her life. Well, it is time for you to discover that purpose, and fulfill it with everything you have.

Many of the difficulties we endure in life are closely tied to our egos. One of the ways to effectively cope with our challenges is to start to focus on a mission to positively affect others. It is impossible to worry about yourself when you are actively involved in helping others. Any noble purpose involves selflessness and service to others. As I will share with you in a few moments, your rewards will dwarf your contributions.

First, it is necessary to determine what your noble purpose is. The best way I have found to do this is to go somewhere where you can be quiet and alone for an hour. Once alone, start to think about the attributes with which you have been blessed, and how they can be used to help others. During this quiet hour, contemplate, meditate, pray, or perform whatever mental process works for you to determine your special talent, and how to use it as a noble purpose. Continue this practice of solitude over time until you come to realize your purpose. Once you come to a conclusion as to what it is, go with it and believe it is a correct assumption. You see, it doesn't matter if it is not completely correct, as it will be close. Once you have a noble purpose, no matter what it is, wonderful results will manifest themselves.

Let me tell you how Zors determined his noble purpose, and how he uses it on a day-to-day basis.

Perhaps it will help you more fully understand the process.

One day Al, a friend of Zors, was describing his new job. He was saying that his company had a mission statement and what a silly concept that was. Many large companies have mission statements that have long been forgotten by their employees. What good is a mission statement if the employees don't remember it, and haven't embraced it as an integral part of their daily activities?

This set Zors to thinking. While mission statements for companies are often no more than public relations gimmicks, what about a personal mission statement to which a person is committed? It is surely true that all of us have a mission in life, so why not discover it and develop a mission statement to be used as an affirmation? Then, in reality, this affirmation is a vehicle by which one can bring his mission, or more accurately, his noble purpose, to life.

Zors did a lot of thinking and praying to discover, within himself, what his noble purpose and mission statement should be. Through this process, he came to realize that his mission statement should reflect two of his strongest attributes. First, he was blessed with the ability to make people laugh. Second, he has a deep spiritual love for mankind. Once he realized this, his noble purpose and mission statement were pretty easy. I hear him every morning and evening carefully reciting his affirmation, which, of course, is his mission statement reflecting his noble purpose. Zors uses his toothbrush as a memory hook to affirm his mission statement before brushing his teeth. Twice a day, from the bathroom, I hear him say, "I will make the world a better place through laughter and love."

Zors has used his mission statement as a tool to leading a life with a noble purpose. I think his contribution to the world is considerable, but his reward for leading a life with a noble purpose far outweighs his contributions.

Think about how the effect of actively living this way can dramatically change your life. First, you do not get bogged down in feeling sorry for yourself, no matter what goes wrong. You are too busy seeking ways to serve your noble purpose. Second, having a noble purpose means you are leading a noble life. No matter what else happens, what you are doing is important. You are important. Your life has meaning. Third, sending out those kinds of ripples always results in attracting wonderful, positive, incoming ripples.

The way you live your life reflects your self-esteem. It is easy to spot someone with low self-esteem, as he reflects it in his appearance and surroundings. Getting into the habit of leading a noble life will elevate your self-worth like nothing else. This will be reflected in your appearance, surroundings, and contentment with life.

Let me tell you a story. A good man died and appeared before the pearly gates. St. Peter was there to greet him and said, "You have led a good life. You have the choice to live in Heaven or Hell. I will accompany you as we visit both places. This way you can make an informed decision."

First they went to Hell and stood before two giant doors. St. Peter opened the doors and exposed the largest dining room ever seen. It was beautiful, with wonderful music and a banquet table that went on forever. There were millions of people sitting on each side of the table, which offered the very finest foods imaginable. There were main courses, salads, soups, desserts, the finest wines ever bottled—a fantastic feast.

The man then noticed that all the people were crying, sobbing, moaning, whining, expressing great despair. When he looked more closely, he saw that all the people's arms were straight, as their elbows did not bend, so they could not partake of the feast. The sadness was overwhelming.

Next they visited Heaven. Again there were two giant doors that, when opened, exposed a very similar scene. There was the great hall with wonderful food and drink, but this time the people were happy. Everyone was laughing, singing, having great fellowship. When the man looked more closely, he discovered that all these people had elbows that would not bend, just like in Hell. The difference here, however, was they were feeding each other.

Your life has a noble meaning to it. You will come to realize that happiness is not the absence of challenges, but the progressive realization of a noble purpose. The glow of your being outshines every star! Discover your noble purpose, commit to it, and experience something more special than you could ever imagine.

—

Ruth Zors entertained no questions after her remarks. It didn't matter, though: the code of silence had been broken.

If You Enjoyed *The Millionaire's Message*, Then You'll Also Enjoy...

The first — and only — traditionally published book by the legendary Five Hundred Million Dollar Man, J.F. (Jim) Straw, whose business activities have generated over $500,000,000 in revenues. In *Mustard Seeds, Shovels, & Mountains*, Mr. Straw explains how he used what he calls "Physio-Psychic Power" to achieve such incredible success.

A #1 Best Seller on Amazon.com!

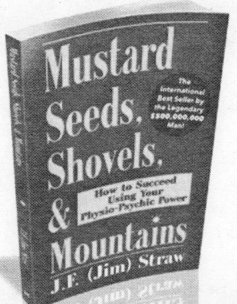

"Anyone who wants to improve their position, succeed at their dreams, truly help others, etc. needs to READ THIS BOOK!!! (sorry to shout, but I really feel this way.)"
–Amazon.com Reviewer

10% OFF YOUR NEXT BOOK!
Use Coupon Code: **ZORS15**

www.ALLISTIpublishing.com

www.KALLISTIpublishing.com

READ.

SUCCEED.

BEAUTIFUL.

10% OFF YOUR NEXT BOOK!
Use Coupon Code: **ZORS15**

READ DAILY. IMPROVE WEEKLY. SUCCEED ALWAYS.

#ReadSucceedBeautiful

www.KALLISTIpublishing.com

About the Author

Bryan A. James is the author of the international best-selling book, *The Parable of the Homemade Millionaire,* a book the legendary Charlie "Tremendous" Jones called "a great little book to build a better life for yourself and your family." Mr. James has held management and executive positions in both the finance and healthcare industries for over thirty-five years and has been president of three different companies that are still active and flourishing today. He is an award-winning salesman and manager who has been responsible for the professional development of hundreds of people.

Mr. James has been recognized, on many occasions, for his outstanding contributions to local charitable organizations and has served on several of their boards of trustees. He is a past-president and a lifetime honorary member of the board of trustees of The Epilepsy Association of Northeast Ohio and a recipient of their prestigious 2004 Legacy Award.

Through many years of intense personal research, he has refined methodologies which are highly effective in assisting anyone in finding lasting success, happiness and peace of mind. Mr. James is a certified hypnotherapist and a member of American Mensa.